The Telephone

Uses and Abuses

Gina Strazzabosco
Moira Reynolds

THE ROSEN PUBLISHING GROUP, INC.

NEW YORK

Published in 1994 by The Rosen Publishing Group, Inc.
29 East 21st Street, New York, NY 10010

First Edition
Copyright 1994 by The Rosen Publishing Group, Inc.

Manufactured in the United States of America

Library of Congress Cataloging-in-Publication Data

Strazzabosco, Gina.
    The telephone: uses and abuses / Gina Strazzabosco & Moira Reynolds. —
1st ed.
    (The Lifeskills library)
    Includes bibliographical references and index.
    ISBN 0-8239-1608-1
    1. Telephone—Juvenile literature. 2. Telephone etiquette—Juvenile
literature. [1. Telephone. 2. Telephone etiquette. 3. Etiquette.] I. Reynolds,
Moira Davison. II. Title. III. Series: Lifeskills library.
TK6165.S77 1993
384.6—dc20   93-25717
                                                       CIP
                                                       AC

CONTENTS

TELEPHONE TECHNOLOGY

At first glance, this book seems to cover a device so common that it needn't have been written about. On the contrary, there is much to learn about the telephone. At least, there was for me. Words like installation, speed dialing, and voice mail had no meaning for me. I had no idea how expensive it is to turn on a phone line, or even that you had to turn it on. Do you know how much an actual phone costs? Or how many kinds there are? Or how to call relatives overseas? Or how to respond to obscene phone calls or get rid of telemarketers? Neither did I. It was amazing to find out exactly how much I didn't know about this ordinary instrument that I use every day.

It would be difficult for today's teenager to imagine life without the telephone.

"Hey Mom, the phone's out," Tallie said. "The storm must have taken down the phone lines. I was expecting a call about a job I interviewed for. I hope they realize what happened and call me tomorrow. The phone should be back on by then, right?"

"I certainly hope so," Mrs. Booker replied. "Your brother was going to call me for a ride home when band practice was over. Now I'll have to wait for him in the parking lot. What a waste of an afternoon." Mrs. Booker picked up a paperback book for the long wait and drove off to the high school.

Tallie's father came home shortly afterward. She kissed him hello and said, "Dad, what are you doing home so early? I thought you were still on night duty at the hospital."

"It was a slow night. The hospital didn't need all of us. I was put on call so I could come home and have dinner with my family for a change. They'll call me on the beeper if they need me." Dr. Booker started toward his bedroom to change clothes for his first night home in several weeks.

"Dad, I hate to disappoint you, but the storm knocked out the phone." Dr. Booker turned around, kissed his daughter goodbye, and headed back to the hospital.

Tallie flopped down on the couch and began doing her homework. She was in the middle of math when she realized that it was too quiet. She put on her favorite CD, but that didn't fill the void. It was the phone. There were no phone calls. She couldn't call her boyfriend, José, or her best friend, Suzanne. She

ALEXANDER GRAHAM BELL

The famous company that was called "Ma Bell" was named for Alexander Graham Bell. He was born in Scotland in 1847. He had a little schooling, but he taught himself most of what he knew about sound. He also learned from his father, who specialized in public speaking and speech correction.

The Bell family emigrated to Canada. In 1872 Alexander opened a school for the deaf. He later became a professor at Boston University.

In his spare time, Alexander worked to figure out what kind of instrument could send several telegraphic messages over one wire at the same time. In 1874 Alexander described his idea for such an instrument to his father. That was a rough outline of the first telephone.

Two years later, Alexander discovered that electrical waves could transmit sound over wire. His discovery was a breakthrough. He applied for a patent on the telephone, but he had more work to do.

The historic moment came on March 10, 1876, when Alexander Graham Bell transmitted his own voice. He said, "Watson, come here; I want you." And he was clearly heard by his assistant. Bell was only 29 years old, and he had changed the world.

wouldn't be taking any messages, or yelling at her brother to finish his call so she could make hers. Tallie felt very isolated. "I'm glad this is only for one night," she muttered.

Bridging the Miles

The telephone. It's tough to imagine life without it. Telephones are everywhere: in your home, at work, in cars, even in briefcases. More than 93 percent of households in the United States have telephone service. Hundreds of millions of calls are made each day. Today many people take the convenience of such easy communication for granted, but the telephone is not very old. Alexander Graham Bell invented the first model about 150 years ago. What do you think he would say about cellular phones?

Telephones are extremely useful. For teenagers, their most common use is for keeping in touch with family and friends, but people rely on telephones for many things. They call to get help in emergencies, to do business, and to get information.

Hotlines

Josh nervously rubbed his hands. He took a deep breath, then picked up the phone. He dialed 1-800-662-HELP.

"National Institute on Drug Abuse. Can I help you?

"Yeah. I, um, I think my brother is a drug addict."

"Well, you called the right place. What makes you think he is addicted?"

"He used to be cool. You know, fun to hang out with. He did pretty well in school. He was even on the

Office Desk Telephone

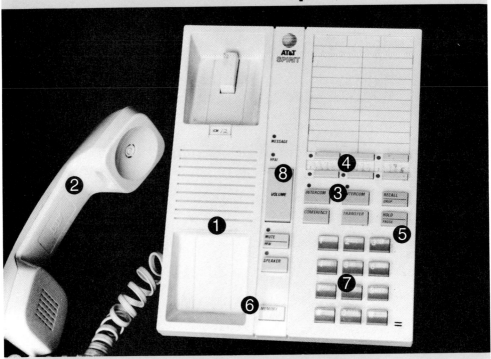

1. Cradle
2. Receiver/handset
3. Intercom buttons
4. indicator lights for incoming calls
5. Hold/pause button
6. Memory button
7. Push buttons for touchtone dialing
8. Volume control

varsity football team, but he quit this year. Now he's failing most of his classes. He hardly ever goes to school. He's always borrowing money from me or stealing from my mom's purse. He has really bad mood swings."

"How old is your brother?"

"Seventeen."

"How long has he been behaving like this?"

"About a year."

"All right. Here's what you do. Call 1-800-662-2255. That's a confidential drug-dependence hotline number. Tell them what you told me. They'll ask you

9

*more questions about you, your brother, and your
family. Then they'll tell you what you can do to help
your brother and yourself. Everything will be okay.
You are a brave person to have called us. You must
love your brother a lot."*

*"Yeah, I guess. Thanks for your help. I feel better
just having said it out loud."*

*"Good luck, and call back if you need any other
information."*

*Josh hung up, relieved that the call was over. One
more to make.*

The hotline is a telephone service that has proved
to be very helpful. There are hotlines for nearly
every problem: AIDS, drug and alcohol use and
abuse, STDs, pregnancy, abortion, and runaways.
Hotlines generally have toll-free 800 numbers.
That means the caller is not charged for the call.
The hotline will answer questions and give you any
information you need.

Emergencies

Another useful service is the national emergency
telephone number, **911**, in the U.S. and Canada.
You can call this number if there is a fire, an accident, or a gas leak, if someone needs an ambulance,
or in any other emergency. It will put you in touch
with an operator who will ask you what is the
trouble, where it is, and your name, address, and
phone number. The operator will then notify the

service needed. For example, in the case of a fire, the nearest fire station will be called.

The 911 number should only be used in an emergency. Being locked out of your house is not an emergency. Someone breaking into your house is. A stranger in the neighborhood is not an emergency. A hit-and-run accident is. Use good judgment if and when you dial 911.

Toll-free 800 Numbers

Toll-free numbers are used for several purposes. Service businesses like mail-order companies, hotels, airlines, Ticketron, and subscription services have toll-free numbers to make ordering easy. Most national offices, nonprofit organizations, and hotlines have 800 numbers to give information and counseling free. AT&T publishes an annual directory that lists all businesses having 800 numbers.

Telephones have greatly increased the speed and ease with which we can communicate. But the telephone, like any other tool, can be abused. In the next few chapters you will learn how to get the most out of the many kinds of telephones and the services that telephone companies offer. You will also discover how the telephone can be abused, and how to avoid such abuses as telemarketing scams and 900 numbers.

Piano
$49.95

$179.95

$269.95

$229.95

THE MANY FACES OF THE TELEPHONE

The telephone is just the tip of the telecommunications iceberg. It extends far beyond the heavy, black, rotary-dial phone your parents probably grew up using. The most basic telephone is the corded phone, and even it comes in many shapes, sizes, and styles.

Corded Phones

The corded phone is the familiar desk or wall phone. Some older models may have a rotary dial, but most have a push-button, or touch-tone, dial. This style of phone may have several features. These are described in Chapter 4.

Office phones usually have special features. Most have several lines for taking or making calls. The

---

Telephones for business or pleasure come in a large variety of shapes, sizes, colors, and special features.

speakerphone enables several people in a room to engage in a conversation. The intercoms allow calls to be made to other offices in the same building. Transferring allows called to be moved from one line or one intercom to another. Conference calling enables three or more people on several phone lines to converse.

Cordless Phones

The cordless phone is like the corded phone, but without the wire connecting the handset, or receiver, to the base. The handset, which runs on a rechargeable battery, can be as far away as 1,000 feet from the base and still place and receive calls. Some handsets can be left off the base for up to a week, but they need to be replaced occasionally to recharge.

Pocket Pagers/Beepers

With the electronic revolution in the late 1970s came the extension of telecommunication. Pocket pagers, or beepers, are small devices equipped with radio receivers. They make a beeping sound when someone is calling. Some even show the number of the person calling. At first beepers were expensive. They were mostly used by professional people. Today they are used by anyone who wants to be reachable at all times. The most complex beepers can be used anywhere in the world.

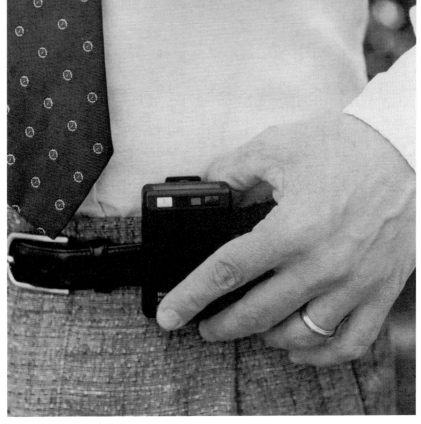

Beepers on the market today are not only used to sound an alert, but can also display a brief message.

Modems

The next development was the modem. A modem is a computer-to-telephone hookup through which information can be sent from one computer to another over a telephone line. Anything that can be seen on a screen can be sent by modem. That includes drawings, charts, newspaper and magazine articles, photographs, documents, and bank and medical records. You can also get information by modem. If you have software like Compuserve for your personal computer, you can access all kinds of references, travel information, up-to-the-minute news reports, and stock information, to name just a few types of information available.

Fax Machines

The facsimile, or fax, machine sends a physical copy of any piece of paper over telephone lines. Items that once had to be mailed or hand delivered are now transmitted almost instantly by fax.

Cellular Telephones

Cellular phones are portable wireless telephones with short-range radio receivers and transmitters. Some 8.9 million people subscribe to cellular service. The cost of the phone has gone down from $2,000 in 1991 to less than $300 today. The latest models are only a few inches long, but very dependable. They can be used almost anywhere.

In fact, cellular phones have become so powerful that questions have been asked about their safety because of the electromagnetic radiation. Some people are concerned that long-term use may cause brain cancer because the phone is held close to the head. According to the Food and Drug Administration, there is no *proof* of a health danger, but some evidence that it is *possible*.

To many people, cellular phones have drawbacks. The ringing and one-sided conversations may bother people in places like museums, libraries, and theaters. Cellular phones can be a great modern convenience, but they break down still another wall between private space and public space.

—

For the price of a phone call, the fax machine can send a copy of any printed matter almost anywhere in the world.

CHAPTER 3

PRACTICAL PHONE SKILLS

The most valuable phone skill is good manners. Remember that the person on the other end of the line cannot see you. Your voice and choice of words create the impression you give. Something as simple as ordering a pizza can be a good or bad experience for people at both ends of the line. The following are two examples of possible conversations. Which one would you say was acceptable?

"Gino's Pizzeria. This is Kim speaking. How may I help you?"

"Hi, Kim. I'd like to order a pizza for delivery, please."

"Sure. May I have your name, address, and phone number?"

Using the telephone directory can save you time and effort.

"*My address is 25 Rocky Boulevard, near Main Street, and my phone number is 555-9084. The name is Max.*"

"*Thanks, Max. What would you like to order?*"

"*I'd like a large pizza, half with mushrooms, half with pepperoni. And three sodas, please.*"

"*Okay. Would you like anything else?*"

"*No, thank you.*"

"*Your total is $13.75. That will be about half an hour. Thanks for calling Gino's Pizzeria.*"

"*Thanks. Bye.*"

"*Yeah?*"

"*Is this the Shepard residence?*"

"*Yeah.*"

"*Is Mr. Frank Shepard there?*"

"*No.*"

"*Do you know when he'll be back?*"

"*Nope.*"

"*May I leave a message?*"

"*Yeah, I guess. Hold on a minute. I've gotta find a pen. No, wait. Let me get some paper.*" She reaches for a napkin. "*Go ahead.*"

"*This is Stephen Katz. My number is 555-2486. I'm calling about an interview he wanted to do. He's got the interview if he calls me by tomorrow morning. Please be sure to give him the message.*"

"*I wouldn't have written it down if I wasn't going to give it to him.*"

"*Fine. Thank you. Goodbye.*" As he hangs up, he thinks sarcastically, "*Nice kid.*"

"Right. Bye, jerk." She leaves the napkin on the table and goes upstairs to finish her homework. Her younger brother comes home. He makes himself a sandwich and grabs the napkin, not noticing the writing on the other side. Assuming that her father found the napkin, she never mentions the call to him. Her father never calls Stephen Katz back and loses his chance at a once-in-a-lifetime interview.

The first conversation may be a little stiff, but it is polite, and both parties are satisfied. In the second conversation, both parties are unhappy with the outcome. There are basic good telephone manners that everyone should be aware of and use.

When you answer the phone, be polite. Most people answer, "Hello?" If answering the phone at a friend's house, some people give the friend's last name: "Hello, McCabe residence."

At home, if an unidentified or unfamiliar caller asks for your mother, but she's still at work or out doing errands, you say, "I'm sorry, she is busy right now" or "I'm sorry, she can't come to the phone right now. May I take a message?" These responses are polite, but also safe. You don't want to let a stranger know when you are alone in the house. If the caller asks when she'll be back, give the information. If the person wants to leave a message, take the name, number, reason for calling, and any other information. Repeat the message back to be sure you have it recorded correctly, and tell the caller you will have your mother return the call as soon as she can.

Next, give your mother the message. Writing it down is only half the job. Be sure to tell her about the call. Some families keep a pad of paper and a pen or pencil by the phone. If yours doesn't, you might want to start the tradition. It saves time.

At a business, always answer with the name of the business. Some people add their name, like Kim at Gino's Pizzeria. Adding, "Good morning" or "Good afternoon" makes the greeting more friendly. When more than one line is ringing, ask the first caller to hold, then answer the second call. Now you can either ask the second caller to hold and continue with the first caller, or find out what the second needs. If it's something quick, such as asking to be connected to another extension or leaving a message, complete the call, then go back to the first.

It is also important to note the date and time of the call and to be sure of the name and number of the caller. It can be very embarrassing for an employer to try to return a call to Mr. Stone using Mrs. James's phone number. Be sure to get the message to the proper person as soon as possible.

When you make a call, have all the information you need right in front of you. If you want to order Chinese food, know exactly what you are ordering before you call. It can be helpful to have the menu at hand. When ordering from a catalog, know the number of the article you're ordering, the page on

---

The car phone enables people to stay in touch with business matters or family.

which it appears, the size, the color, and the price.
Have your credit card number available.

Displaying good telephone manners is more than
common courtesy. It makes life easier. People are
nice to you if you are nice to them—even on the
phone.

Other Skills

Now that you know all about proper phone manners, here are some other practical skills.

Telephone Books

As you probably know, there are two kinds of phone
books: the white pages and the yellow pages. The
white pages contain local residential listings; county,
state, and federal government office listings; and
often an alphabetical listing of businesses. Other
information, such as time zones, area codes, and the
current calling rates are also given. The yellow
pages list businesses alphabetically by the kind of
product or service provided.

Directory Assistance

More than 90 percent of calls made in the United
States are local. If you don't know the number you
want to call, you can look it up in a phone book and
dial it directly. If you don't have a phone book, you
can call directory assistance. Dial 411 and give the

name of the person or business whose number you want. A computerized voice will tell you the phone number. If you want to speak to the operator again, stay on the line. These calls cost up to 45 cents.

For directory assistance outside your area code, dial 1- (area code of location to be dialed) 555-1212. Area codes in the United States are listed in the front of your phone book. For example, you want to dial directory assistance in Tampa, Florida, from Rochester, New York, but you don't know the area code. The phone book lists the Tampa area code as 813, so you dial 1-813-555-1212. You say you need the number for Sabine's Shoe Store in Tampa. A computerized voice will give you the number. You can stay on the line and ask the operator for the street address of the store. These calls cost up to 60 cents.

Operator Assistance

Some telephone calls require the assistance of an operator.

Collect calls are billed to the number you call. To make a collect call, dial 0. When the operator answers, say you want to make a collect call, then give the phone number. The operator will ask your name and give it to the person who answers the phone. This person must accept the charges before you are allowed to complete the call. Collect calls are nearly twice the cost of regular phone calls.

On *third-party* calls, you call a second party and have it charged to a third. Dial 0 and tell the operator you want to make a call and charge it to a third party. The operator will ring the third party to get an okay of charges, then ring the second party. Third-party calls cost about half again the price of a regular call.

On *person-to-person* long-distance calls, the charge does not begin until a specific person or extension is reached. Most direct long-distance calls are station-to-station calls. The charge begins as soon as the phone is answered.

Calling Cards

Calling cards are telephone credit cards. The cardholder is given a number, usually his home phone number with an extra four digits at the end. Any calls made with this number are charged to his monthly telephone bill. Calling-card calls can be made by direct dial or with operator assistance. For direct dial, dial 0, then the area code and phone number of the person you are calling; wait for a beep, then dial the card number. For operator assistance, dial 0 and tell the operator you want to make a calling-card call. Give the number you're calling and the card number. These calls cost about half again the cost of a regular call. The calling card service can be abused. Read about that in Chapter 5.

Children should be taught at an early age how to make an emergency call.

name, number, time you called, and a brief message, we'll get back to you as soon as we can. Thank you."

It's a bit predictable, but solid. You can be more creative, but remember that people other than your friends will hear your message. Don't leave something like this:

"Yo! On vacation till next week. Leave a message. We'll get back to you".

Being friendly and polite on the phone are important, but so is being safe. Suppose burglars working the neighborhood notice that your house is empty. They call to be sure, get that message, and break in. Believe it or not, this has happened, especially when answering machines first became popular. People should be more careful, saying "We can't get to the phone," rather than "We're not home."

Leaving a Message

Take some time to think about the message you will leave if you get an answering machine at the number you call. Usually answering machine tapes only hold a few minutes' worth of messages. If you ramble on for too long, chances are no one else will be able to leave a message. Your message should be brief and spoken in a slow, clear voice. Give your name, number, the day and time you called, and your message.

For instance:

"Hello. It's 3 o'clock on Wednesday, and this is a message for Jen. This is Sandy Hayn and I need to find out what time basketball practice is tomorrow. Please call me back at 555-8740. Thank you."

It is more clear than:

"Hi, it's me. Call me back about practice time tomorrow. Talk to you later. Bye."

Answering machines can be a great asset to any home or business, provided they are used properly at both ends of the line.

Wrong Numbers

About 15 percent of all telephone calls are wrong numbers. If you happen to be the caller, don't hang up on the person who answers. No one likes to be hung up on. Tell them you dialed the wrong number, apologize for the disturbance, and then hang up.

If you happen to answer a wrong number, be polite—even if you've been dragged out of bed. Ask what number is wanted, then say this is not it. As a matter of safety, *never* give your name or number. If the caller asks, say, "Who is this, please?" Most likely the caller will apologize and hang up. If not, say again that it is the wrong number, and hang up.

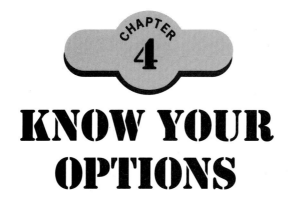

KNOW YOUR OPTIONS

So many plans and services are available that it can be difficult to choose which one best suits your needs. Rates and services vary. Here are some of the most common choices.

Basic Monthly Service

Installation means turning on the phone line in your home. This can cost $80 or more. You can pay the charge all at once, or divide it over a period of up to twelve months.

Measured service is inexpensive and includes about 50 local calls per month.

Flat-rate service costs a little more than measured service, and includes 400 local calls a month. You pay the going rate for additional calls.

Information about dialing local and out-of-town calls is usually found on the front of all public phones.

Long-Distance Service

Several companies offer long-distance and international calling service. The largest companies are AT&T, Sprint, and MCI. They offer different rates for different plans. For AT&T, call 1-800-222-0300; for Sprint, call 1-800-877-7746; for MCI, call 1-800-777-5555.

Phone Lines

Suppose the phone book lists Diaz, Heather. That means there is a phone line into Ms. Diaz's house. She pays a specific rate for that line. No matter how many extensions (phones) she has on that line, the rate is the same. Some houses have extensions on every floor, including the basement or even the garage. The charge for the line does not include actual telephones. Those you must purchase yourself. A basic corded phone costs anywhere from $30 to $50, and a cordless around $75.

If you see under Cerar, Anna, "Children's Phone," it means that household has a second line with a different number. There is an extra monthly rate for the second line.

Custom Calling Services

Many custom calling services are available. With the speed of today's technology, the number of services is constantly increasing.

Most services have an initial connection charge as well as a monthly charge.

Call Waiting lets you know someone else is calling while you're using your phone. You will hear a beep tone. If you ignore the first beep, you'll hear a second one in ten seconds. The party calling you hears only the normal ringing. If you want to answer, put the first caller on hold by pressing the receiver button once. The second call is automatically transferred to you. To get back to the first caller, push the receiver button again. It is possible to disconnect call waiting if you don't want to be disturbed by beeps. You can also just ignore them.

On the flip side, if you are calling someone who you know has call waiting, and the person doesn't answer it, don't call back repeatedly. Chances are the person is ignoring it for a good reason. Try calling back a little later.

Call Forwarding transfers incoming calls to a different number, even in another state. You can still make outgoing calls when this is operating; however, you cannot answer incoming calls. The cost of the call from your phone to the number to which the call is forwarded is billed to your home phone.

Touch-tone dialing lets you place calls almost instantly, unlike rotary, or pulse, dialing.

Distinctive Ringing lets you recognize calls from certain numbers by a special ring. For instance, when the phone rings twice in quick succession, you know it's your girlfriend.

Automatic Callback enables you to return the last call received, whether or not you answered it. If that line is busy, this service will continue to dial for 30 minutes, or until the line is free.

Call Screening blocks calls from certain numbers. Screened callers hear an announcement that the number dialed is not taking calls at the moment.

Caller ID can be a valuable service if you have obscene phone calls, or if you like to screen your calls before answering. After the first ring, the number of the caller is displayed. You can then decide whether or not to answer the call. If it turns out to be an obscene call, you can report the number to your phone company or the police.

Voice Mail is an automatic answering service run by the phone company. Callers can leave messages when no one answers or when the phone is in use. The messages are retrieved by dialing your phone number and a password.

Repeat Dialing automatically redials a number when a busy signal is reached.

Speed Calling lets you reach frequently called local or long distance numbers by dialing only one or two digits.

Three-Way Calling (Conference Call) lets you add a third party to your existing conversation without operator assistance.

Personal 800 numbers are useful for people whose children or families live far away. All calls made on the 800 number are charged to the person who ordered the number.

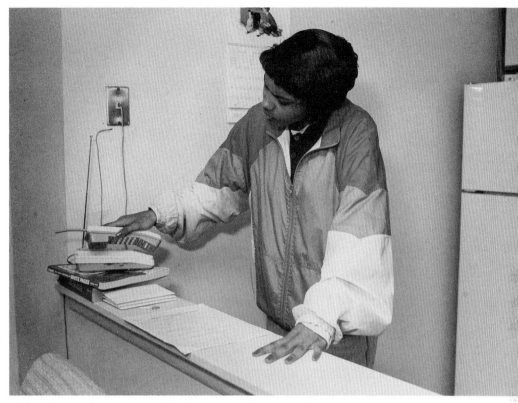

It is wise to hang up quickly on an obscene call rather than engage in any conversation.

New services, such as international interpreters, are constantly being developed. If you call Japan via AT&T, interpreters will simultaneously interpret from English to Japanese and vice versa. Soon the personal interpreter will be replaced with a computerized interpreter.

Another advance in telephone service is Voice Dialing. People will soon be able to dial a number just by saying the name of the person they want to call. A family will be able to compile a voice directory. You pick up the receiver and say, "Dad." The phone will recognize your voice and dial your father. This service will reduce wrong-number calls. It will also be faster than touch-tone dialing.

USE AND ABUSE

Like any other instrument, the telephone can be abused. The way to avoid such abuse is to know how and why it exists, and how to deal with it.

Telemarketing

Many businesses use the telephone to sell goods and services. Most are honest, but some are not. The Federal Trade Commission estimates that Americans lose $1 billion a year through telemarketing scams. Offers for oil and gas leases, free vacations, rare coins, and health or car insurance are just a few of the scams that have been successfully carried off. Here are some tips that the U.S. Office of Consumer Affairs and the FTC suggest to help you decide whether a telemarketing call is legitimate.

A pleasant telephone manner is important when dealing with customers.

When you are on the phone:

- Ask for the name, address, and phone number of the company calling you.
- Ask for written material to be sent to you.
- Be suspicious if you are pressured to make a purchase.
- Ask for names of satisfied customers.
- Be wary of free merchandise such as prizes.
- Never give your credit card or social security number.

You can call the Better Business Bureau if you want to check on the company that contacted you. You can also report anything suspicious to:

Federal Trade Commission
Telemarketing Fraud Project
6th and Pennsylvania Avenue
Washington, DC 20580

To get rid of unwanted sales calls, write to:
Telephone Preference Services
Direct Marketing Association
6 East 43rd Street
New York, NY 10017

Unsolicited Calls

Calls promoting surveys, polls, fund-raising, clubs, or other functions can be annoying. The caller usually does all the talking and gives you little chance to respond. This is what happened to Scott.

The phone rang soon after Scott's grandmother's birthday party began. Scott answered and was asked to participate in a study about teenage use of sporting goods. The caller said if he would answer a few questions, he would receive a free camera.

Half an hour later, Scott was still on the phone. He could hear people singing "Happy Birthday." His family had tired of waiting for him.

When the survey was finally over, Scott returned to the dining room just in time to see his brother finish off the last piece of cake. Scott's grandmother was a little disappointed. Worst of all, the camera turned out to be a worthless piece of junk.

Scott could have handled the situation differently. He could have replied, "I'm sorry, but I'm busy at the moment," and hung up. Don't be afraid to take control of the conversation. Don't let the caller keep you on the phone longer than you want to.

Obscene, Harassing, or Threatening Calls

It is illegal to use the phone for any of these kinds of calls. If you receive such calls, do the following:
- Hang up and try to stay calm.
- Keep a record of the date and time of each call. You may need it later if you report the incidents to the police.
- If you are threatened, call the police.
- If other calls continue, report them to the phone company. Most phone books list a number you can call to make such reports.

Illegal Wiretapping

It is illegal to record a phone conversation without the consent of both parties, unless it is done by law-enforcement officers who have permission from a judge. If you hear a beep every 15 seconds, the person to whom you are speaking is recording your conversation. If you do not want this, ask that the recording machine be turned off.

900 Numbers

These numbers are used to sell anything from pornographic conversations to astrological advice. Do you know the actual cost to you as the consumer?

Darren was home on a Friday night as usual. It was partly his own fault. He could never work up the courage to ask Quinn out. Somehow he just couldn't do it. And all his friends had girlfriends.

He plunked down in front of the TV and flipped on MTV. Several hours later, the zillionth commercial came on: "Lonely? You don't have to be. Talk to people your own age just waiting for you to call! Call 1-900-Party4U right now!" In small letters under the number was, "$.95 for the first minute, $.99 for every minute thereafter. Age 18 or older." Darren never noticed that part. He hesitated for a second, then picked up the phone and dialed the party line number. Forty-five minutes later he hung up, went to bed, and dreamed about the girl he'd been talking to.

Darren's call cost $44.51. Do you think that's a high price to pay for a dream? When you call 900 numbers, you are just handing over your money (or your parent's money) to some clever people.

Some 900 numbers can be useful. The Better Business Bureau uses one to sell its services over the phone. There is a 24-hour consultation service on medication called "Ask the Pharmacist." These are helpful, but remember that most 900 calls cost more than they're worth.

Calling Cards and Fraud

As mentioned earlier, calling cards are a convenient way of charging a phone call to your bill. But like credit cards, they can easily be abused. Don't over-use the card. Use good judgment. Realize that it is a privilege to have the card.

Another form of abuse is stealing and selling calling card numbers. The thief waits by a pay phone for someone to use a calling card. Then he watches to see what number is pressed for the calling card. Or he stands farther away and looks through binoculars to see the number. He later sells that number. He may sell it to someone who can't afford to call his or her family in another country or someone who makes a lot of out-of-state calls. The person calls from a pay phone, and talks as long and as often as he or she wants. The caller cannot be traced. The thief is long gone. The fraud continues. The only person who loses is the owner of the calling card. All calls made with his number are charged to his phone bill.

To avoid the theft of your number, make sure no one is standing close to the phone you are calling from. Cover the buttons with your free hand when you press in your number, or else dial the operator and give your number quietly.

Conclusion

It is nearly impossible for us to imagine a time when the world operated without telephones. Advanced technology continues to add new communication services. As phone users, we need to be kept informed about such developments. We need to understand how these developments affect our society and how they affect us.

Telephones will continue to change in your lifetime. There will always be something new to learn about them. It may be a new voice-dial service or a monitor that gives you a lifelike image of the caller. Make the most of the technology that brings the world to your door. Learn how to use a modem at your school or library to access information. Try out your new long-distance calling skills. Keep up with the health watch on cellular phones. Tell your parents about some of the services that you think might make life a little easier. Put a pad of paper and a pen by every telephone in the house.

If you still are not convinced that the telephone is an incredible instrument, imagine life without it.

GLOSSARY

EXPLAINING NEW WORDS

access The ability to get into and to use.

computerized Created with the use of a computer.

confidential Meant to be kept secret.

modem A device that converts data for transmission by telephone to a computer.

radiation The process by which energy is transmitted from one body to another.

rechargeable Able to be charged again with electricity.

residential Referring to a person's home.

scam A swindle or way of cheating.

screen To accept or refuse a call or visitor.

software Programs for directing a computer how to operate.

technology Knowledge of science and how to put it to use.

telecommunication The sending of information over long distances by electronic signals.

transmit To send to a person or a place.

FOR FURTHER READING

Boettinger, H.M. *The Telephone Book: Bell, Watson, Vail, and American Life, 1876-1983,* rev. ed. New York: Stearn Publications, 1983.

Boynton, J. *Answering Machine Etiquette.* South Houston, TX: Astro-Art Enterprises, 1987.

Farrell, T.J. *Effective Telephone Skills.* San Diego, CA: Harcourt Brace Jovanovich, 1989.

Klein, J.H. *The Phone Book.* Virginia Beach, VA: The Donning Co., 1987.

Weiss, D.H. *Winning on the Telephone.* New York: American Management Association, 1988.

INDEX

About the Authors

Gina Strazzabosco received a BA in Liberal Studies from the State University of New York at Stony Brook and took an intensive four-week course at the Denver Publishing Institute. She now works as an editor and free-lance writer. Ms. Strazzabosco lives in New York City.

Moira Reynolds is a free-lance writer with several books to her credit. She has contributed to magazines and newspapers and often teaches an adult education course in writing nonfiction for publication. Ms. Reynolds lives with her husband in Marquette, Michigan.

Photo Credits
Cover: All photos by Dru Nadler
Pages 17 and 19: Blackbirch Graphics, Inc.; all other photos by Dru Nadler.

Design/Production by Blackbirch Graphics, Inc.